THE CHANGING FACE OF NEWBURY

THE CHANGING FACE OF NEWBURY

Tony Higgott

with a foreword by Sue Hopson

COUNTRYSIDE BOOKS
NEWBURY BERKSHIRE

First published 2016

COUNTRYSIDE BOOKS
3 Catherine Road
Newbury
Berkshire
RG14 7NA

To view our complete range of books, please visit us at
www.countrysidebooks.co.uk

ISBN 978 1 84674 340 5

Cover photograph of market day in Newbury, 1971
by Jim Irving

Produced through The Letterworks Ltd., Reading
Typeset by KT Designs, St Helens
Printed by Short Run Press Ltd., Exeter

Foreword

Photographs are a good way of showing any reader how things used to look. For those of us who have lived in Newbury for quite a long time, they are an excellent reminder of what the town was like. Tony Higgott's new book has a selection of photographs covering many aspects of Newbury, and illustrating how they have changed in the past 50 or 60 years. In many ways this book builds from the base of what the town was like just after the Second World War, which he described in *Newbury in the 1950s* for the same publisher.

Some of the images make their point almost instantly, whilst others, especially the aerial views, reward detailed study as so much is shown. There are many images of town-centre businesses, but he hasn't forgotten the other ways in which Newburians are employed, for example, engineering still continues its long history. The relatively new businesses such as electronics are now well-established. They bring a whole new, very modern, set of skills to the town. Vodafone has obviously made the greatest impact, not only by the number of staff employed, but also through its Headquarters building at Shaw. It puts the name of Newbury firmly on the international map. Likewise, Newbury Racecourse makes the town's name known by references in the national media. These perhaps make a change from the notoriety of the Greenham and Newbury bypass protests, which, in turn, drew attention to the town in the final decades of the twentieth century.

I am sure all readers will find something of interest in the more than one hundred images that form the core of this book.

Sue Hopson

River Kennet iced over, early 1960s. *David Canning*

CONTENTS

Publisher's Note

Please be aware that the credits against photographs supplied by West Berkshire Museum include their catalogue numbers, and these should not be confused with the date when the photograph was shot.

Market day 1970/71. South-bound traffic mixes with pedestrians. Beynons were trading in clothing and furnishing as they had for almost 150 years and nearby properties were still taking on the form of private dwellings, not shops or restaurants as now. *Jim Irving*

Market Town

From early times, towns were by definition manufacturing and trading centres. Markets and fairs were the means by which buying and selling took place. Over the centuries other types of business were set up to service this trade – mills to grind the corn, merchants to buy the grain, maltings and breweries to use the barley, butchers and abattoirs converting livestock to meat, dairies to process and distribute milk, and banks, solicitors and accountants, architects and surveyors to assist the development of rural and urban businesses. Shops came into being to sell clothing, foodstuffs, furniture and household goods throughout the week – not just on market days. Essentially this was still the role of Newbury in the immediate post 1939-45 war years.

Much of the centre of Newbury can be seen in this photograph taken from the telephone exchange tower by Jim Irving in 1974. Central, is the Town Hall, built for the Borough in the 1870s, with the roof of the Corn Exchange in the foreground and St Nicolas' church to the left. To the right of the church tower is the out-door swimming pool, with its porched entrance. To the right of the photograph, nestling amongst the trees, is Goldwell House, Old Bath Road, whilst below it are the early 19th century terraces of West Street (prior to the building of office blocks and a car park) with the roofs of Elliotts of Newbury's furniture works in between (now Strawberry Hill). Above the National Westminster Bank are the rears of The House Of Toomer (now Clarks) and Boots' premises. *Jim Irving*

At the north-east corner of the Market Place were the auction rooms of Day, Shergold and Herberts (now Slug and Lettuce, formerly The Hogshead) where weekly sales of farm produce and plants were held. Furniture and household effects were sold fortnightly, until the firm's closure in 1988. This photo shows fruit and vegetables being viewed prior to the start of a sale in 1985. *Jim Irving*

Rabbits and hares being displayed by a porter prior to viewing. *Jim Irving*

Shergold's final produce auction with John Hutchings the auctioneer and company director in typical pose, his gavel ready to strike the back of his clipboard to signify completion of the sale of a batch of eggs. *Jim Irving*

The Cattle Market in Market Street closed in June 1969, bringing to an end almost 900 years of livestock sales and, perhaps, symbolising the end of Newbury as a traditional market town. The Corn Exchange continued in business for a few more years, with trading formally ending in 1983. Early in the 20th century there had been 100 merchants' desks arranged in the hall, but by the mid-1950s the number had declined to 24. In its last few years, when it had become little more than a social club for a few of the older farmers and traders, there was just one token desk.

Town Mills, late 1960s. The two principal corn dealers were Midwinters and H Dolton & Son Ltd. The latter firm had been founded as a market gardening business at the end of the 18th century, but by the 1850s had expanded into grain dealing. Initially based at Newbury Wharf, and later Shaw Mill, they purchased Town Mills and West Mills from Hovis McDougall in the later 1950s. *Courtesy of C & H Marriage*

Town Mills from the air, 1971. As grain dealing handled increasingly huge quantities using large lorries, access to the mill and limitations of the buildings, led to Doltons selling their Newbury premises and moving to a purpose-built mill near Hermitage, which was completed in 1972.

Much else of interest can be seen in the photograph, including the bus station at Newbury Wharf, the roof of the Plaza Theatre, with its fly tower next to a few trees at the top centre of the image, and part of the area being cleared for building the Kennet Shopping Mall to the right-hand side. Just below this is the Pearl Assurance building, with its tower still with its original five storeys. The whole Pearl site is now in plans for redevelopment. *Courtesy of C & H Marriage*

Town Mills were demolished soon after Doltons left and for a few years (until flats were built on the site in 1981– see page 39) this view of St Nicolas's church was revealed. The verger's house and church hall can be seen at the right hand side. Offices were built here when St Nicolas built new church halls. *David Canning*

Shaw Mill, 1953, sold by Dolton's around 1960 and used for storage. It was converted to housing in the early 1980's.
West Berkshire Museum 1996.125.14

Charles Midwinter & Son were also long-established corn dealers and this building in Cheap Street was their most public property. It provided grain and seed storage on its upper floors and behind the shop. The two right hand windows of the facade were originally doorways through which sacks could be hoisted. In 1988 Midwinter merged with Lidstones, a Slough-based company. See photo on page 18 for the site of their main corn store and processing facilities. *Courtesy of Alan Vince*

Kimber's Corner (Pound Street and Bartholomew Street). *Jim Irving – West Berkshire Museum D 3995*

There were at least three provision merchants in Newbury who supplied foods to the large country houses and farmers of the area – Wells in Northbrook Street, Forest Stores on Newbury Bridge and Kimber's by Black Boy's Bridge – seen above. One farmer's daughter recalls from the 1950s and 60s that on a Thursday her father would attend the cattle Market, then have lunch at The Dolphin with other farmers. Her mother would drive in separately to do her week's shopping. She would park at Camp Hopsons and leave the Landrover unlocked. Forest Stores would then wheel round her order, previously phoned in, and load it into the vehicle. There were no concerns about theft at that time.

Lloyds bank, The Broadway, 1973/4. From early in the 19th century, local banks were created by groups of wealthy businessmen. Gradually these merged into larger groups and by the late 20th century most banking was provided by 'the big five'. In Newbury these were clustered in the Market Place/Bridge Street area. Smaller branches of the banks were further from the centre to provide for the large amounts of cash and cheques resulting from commercial transactions. With the advent of 'plastic' and, later, electronic banking these branches closed. Lloyds branch shown here closed in the early 1980s and York House was restored to what it may have looked like as a private house. *West Berkshire Museum 2004.50.545*

Newbury Agricultural Show. This is a photograph of the showground entrance in 1981 when the show was held at Shaw. Newbury District Agricultural Society have held annual shows at various sites in the area since their foundation in 1909. In 1984 the Society purchased land for a permanent show ground adjacent to Junction 13 of the M4. The show, held in September, has developed into one of the top ten agricultural shows in the country and is now known as The Royal County of Berkshire Show. *Jim Irving – West Berkshire Museum 2003.46.40*

Newbury Relief Road. Following the building of Western Avenue in the late 1950s, diverting A4 traffic to the north of the town, the next change was the Newbury Relief Road, from St John's Road to what became the Robin Hood Roundabout, begun 1963 and opened September 1965. This required the building of new bridges over the railway and the River Kennet, an embankment along the edge of Victoria Park and a realignment of Cheap Street and Greenham Road. (*Caption continues at top of page 20*)

Communications

Roads, Rail and Words

The second half of the 20th century saw an immense growth in road transport. More people were able to afford a car and the greatly increased range of personal and domestic goods and equipment which became available – for which road transport was the favoured distribution method. A greater volume of produce and goods were imported from and exported to mainland Europe following Britain's joining of the Common Market in January 1973.

Newbury's geographical position brought both advantages and disadvantages. The A4 was the principal route from London to the West, whilst the A34 was the main link between the south coast ports of Southampton and Portsmouth and the population and manufacturing centres of the Midlands and north. Many modification were made to the routes of these roads through the town, to reduce the congestion and delays to local and long-distance transport. The most contentious was the A34 Newbury bypass completed in 1998. For many years the town had been calling for relief from the increasing traffic which clogged the town's roads. In 1982 there was consultation on alternative routes, but in 1984 the Department of Transport announced that it favoured the western route and after public enquiries this route was confirmed in 1994. Opposition to this route through attractive natural landscape had crystallised during the consultation period, but now national organisations such as Friends of the Earth became involved. The opposition reached a peak in 1996 when groups of protestors attempted to stop preparatory clearing work by digging complex tunnels and climbing trees to try and prevent them being felled. One young man, nicknamed 'Swampy', caught attention by going to quite extreme lengths such as living in deep underground holes and being chained to obstacles, to hold up the work. The opposition was the biggest anti-road demonstration in British history and brought massive national and international media interest. The contractors, aided by security guards and police, prevailed and the route was cleared by April 1996.

In past centuries people wanted travellers to pass through their town and make use of its inns, shops and other businesses. The second half of the 20th century brought in a fundamental change whereby most travellers were guided around the edges of towns, though signposting to easily accessible car parks encouraged those who knew they were ready to break their journeys so to do.

Railway and canal use also changed and there were major developments, too, to telephonic and printed means of communication.

(*Continued from page 18*). This photograph shows Victoria Park to the left of the new road, top centre, but it also indicates many other points of interest. In the foreground is Gowrings Garage and showrooms (built for Marchants). Above this and to the right of their car parking area, just south of the railway, is the block of buildings forming Midwinter's main store and seed processing buildings. The other side of the railway, to the right of the road is Berkshire Builders Merchants and right again is the Nias garage and Plenty's metal foundry and then the Newbury Diesel Company's works, below all of these is the railway goods yard. The whole of this site north of the railway is now occupied by Sainsbury's and Mole Country Stores (formerly Scats). Gowrings site and the land north to the railway is now occupied by Burger King, Halfords and Staples. *Courtesy of Alan Vince*

Marchants Garage and deep floods to the A34, c 1966. The photo faces south and today has Burger King on the left and Greenham House, off picture, to the right. The Sandleford Link is not yet built. The Adam and Eve pub is in the background, this was demolished for the building of the Sandleford Link. *David Canning*

Cheap Street Bridge prior to its removal in 1963. The gables seen in the background are those of the Axe & Compass pub, Cheap Street, demolished in 1964 as part of the Relief Road construction. Until Greenham Common airfield was extended in 1950, Cheap Street / Greenham Road had been the main route to Kingsclere and Basingstoke. *West Berkshire Museum 1996.125.76*

Site of Cheap Street Bridge from the railway. The Railway Hotel was demolished in the 1980's *West Berkshire Museum 1995.41.7*

Newbury and the Kennet from the east c 1960, before the A34 bridge was built. *David Canning*

The hatches to the right of the bottom photo opposite now have the premises of the *Newbury Weekly News* to their north and are used to control the volume of water in the K & A Canal. Further towards Newbury Victoria park appears to be fenced off from the canal and the Emergency (American) Bridge can be seen.

A34 road bridge when new, 1966 *David Canning*

The M4 to the north of Newbury opened in 1971, initially removing much east-west traffic from the A4. Six years later a new link was made from the M4 to the Robin Hood roundabout, transferring north-south traffic from Oxford Road. Two years after that in 1979, Newtown Road and St John's Road were relieved by the opening of the Sandleford Link. All these changes moved the cross-roads of the A4/A34 from The Broadway and what is now the Waitrose roundabout, to the Robin Hood roundabout – making it a feature (nicknamed The Kamikaze Roundabout) many local drivers dreaded. Later, changes were made to its layout and traffic lights introduced, making it easier and safer to use.

Greenham Road from the south, early 1970's. Howard Road is joining it from the left and is the point where the Sandleford Link was to split Greenham Road to join the A34. The Adam and Eve pub is at the far end of the houses on the right and the construction of the Telecom tower can be seen in the background. *(photographer not known)*

Pedestrianisation of part of the town centre has been gradually brought in during the past two decades. It now includes Bartholomew Street north of the entrance to the multi-storey car park and continues to the Northbrook Street / West Street corner and includes the Market Place. The area is restricted to pedestrians from 10.00 am until 6.00 pm. Initially, buses and taxis were allowed to use the otherwise pedestrian area, but the replaced Park Way bridge and development of Parkway allowed for the re-routing of buses.

In November 2015 a new road bridge over the railway was opened from the roundabout where Hambridge Lane leaves Hambridge Road, to give improved access to Newbury racecourse and to the housing developments there. *(Author)*

A34 from British Telecom tower 1974.
Payment for the use of Central car park was made at the kiosk at the bend of Wharf Road, while visiting coaches parked adjacent to the River Kennet/K&A Canal. The end of The Granary can just be seen at the left-hand side, opposite to the then public toilets. On the other side of the road there is no sign of the London Road Industrial Estate (though the sewage pumping station and an abattoir were in the area), but Newbury Football Club's ground is established. It is interesting to note, in view of the access now being created from the A339 to the Faraday Road redevelopment, that the football club had a direct access road in 1974. *Jim Irving*

In the 1960s several large car parks were created (in addition to established areas such as Park Way) especially in the area of the museum and Newbury Relief road. When the bus station moved from Newbury Wharf in the mid-1970s to a purpose-built facility on the corner of Market Street and Bartholomew Street, more space for parking was released, as it was a decade later when the council's engineers department moved from the south side of The Granary. A multi-storey car park was built in the mid-1960s on the site of the Cattle Market, but this in turn was demolished twenty years later to allow the creation of a new bus station. This was needed as Phase III of the Kennet Centre saw the extension of Sainsburys store and erection of a new multi-storey car park on the 1970s site. In the interim the bus station moved back to Newbury Wharf. In 2016 development plans for the area between Market Street and Newbury Train Station include the bus station which is scheduled to move for the fourth time in forty years to a third site off Wharf Road!

1985. The multi-storey car park, Market Street, looking eastwards. *Jim Irving – West Berkshire Museum 1995.65.12*

1986. The same multi-storey car park in Market Street under demolition. Nobody was too sorry, one of the reasons being that the upper floors had a slight tilt which could cause filled shopping trolleys to move off downhill away from one's car. *Jim Irving – West Berkshire Museum 1995.65.13*

The Bus Station in the 1960s when it was at Newbury Wharf. The end of the Granary can be seen far left of picture *(photographer not known)*

The Bus Station in the 1970s in Market Street. Behind the wide open space is Bartholomew Street. *West Berkshire Museum 2003.46.11*

Bus Station, Market Street, 2016. *(publisher)*

The official opening by councillor Tony Steele in July 1989 of a multi-storey car park in Pembroke Road, behind and to the west of Northbrook Street. *Peter Bloodworth – West Berkshire Museum 2008.21.1*

The Parkway Shopping Centre, overlooking Victoria Park to the east, opened in late 2011. It incorporates a two-level underground car park, more than replacing the surface car parking previously on its site.

Railways

From the end of the 19th century, in addition to the GWR west country main line, Newbury had served as a junction station, with bays to each platform on the opposite side to the main line. The Didcot, Newbury and Winchester line joined the main line just west of Boundary Road and left it again at Enborne. The station was also a terminus of the Lambourn Branch line which ran alongside the main line to the west, then turned north through Speen, truncating Craven Road. Passenger traffic on the former line ceased in the early 1960's and the line closed completely in 1966. Regular passenger traffic to Lambourn ended in 1960, but the line to Welford Park, servicing the American air force munitions depot, remained in use until the end of 1973.

There had been a busy goods yard to the east of the Relief Road, with sidings serving Newbury Diesel Company and the gasworks. As transport of more goods transferred to road and the gasworks was made redundant by the introduction of natural gas in the 1960s (when a new gasholder was erected in Hambridge Road), the yard closed. Now part of Sainsbury's and Mole Country Stores are on its site.

In July 2009 the Government announced that several railway lines would be electrified, including the line from Reading to Newbury. A revised schedule in 2016 stated that the Newbury line would be completed by December 2018. Work has been carried out to the road bridges in the area, several having been rebuilt and others altered to allow headroom for the overhead electric cables. Boundary Road bridge caused major difficulties with the road closed to through traffic for more than 12 months.

The Didcot line branching north and passing under Hambridge Road bridge, early 1960s. *David Canning*

Diesel railcar on the Lambourn branch 1950s, Bartholomew Street bridge in the background, the rear of houses in St Michael Road to the left *(photographer not known)*

Railway Goods Yard from the south, 1960. The first truck of the goods train on the mainline is loaded with coal. At that date coal was widely used as a fuel for domestic fires and commercial energy. The goods shed, where a wide range of packages were unloaded or loaded, is prominent and maltings buildings can be seen to the left of St Nicolas' tower. *David Canning*

Newbury Station in 1973. Passengers are near a west-bound train whilst an express passes through Newbury on its way to London. Both are diesel hauled, diesel having replaced steam engines in the 1960s. Notice also the Semaphore signal, long since replaced by coloured light signals. *David Canning*

The Canal

The Kennet and Avon Canal Association had fought against any final closure of the canal during the 1950s, but in 1962 it became the Kennet and Avon Canal Trust with the aim of raising money and coordinating volunteer labour to restore it. Section by section the canal was again made navigable, but a final boost was given by a very large National Lottery grant which enabled the waterway to be made usable for its whole length from Reading to Bath. In 1990 it was officially opened by The Queen. During the intervening 30 years, rather than commercial transport, the canal had been used for leisure purposes – short boat trips and rowing boat hire. It is now part of the major network of inland waterways extensively used by leisure boat owners and hirers. There are three marinas in Newbury where boats can be kept and maintained.

A major figure in the battles to save the canal was a Newbury man, John Gould. In the late 1940s he had bought a pair of narrow boats and began to develop a carrying business. His predicament when the canal was threatened with closure was used as the basis of the legal appeal. For the rest of his life John worked to ensure the sympathetic restoration of the waterway and its environs.

Lock Cottage and Newbury Lock, looking very rural. John Gould used to say it brought the countryside into the town centre. *Jack Hole – West Berkshire Museum 1999.11.29*

Eight of John Gould's rowing boats for hire, with his 'floating office', by Victoria Park about 1960 – before the relief road bridge. *David Canning*

The *Newbury Weekly News*

The *Newbury Weekly News* remains one of the leading independent regional newspapers in the country. It began its publication in 1867 from 34 Northbrook Street, where it remained until 1982. In January of that year it began publishing from modern, much larger, premises in Faraday Road. Three years later a new printing machine enabled the paper to be printed in full colour.

Phones and Vodafone

Operator (left) at the manual switchboard of Newbury Telephone Exchange, 1974. *(Brian Burgess)*

The local telephone system operated with a manual switchboard for long-distance calls until 1975, when the new automatic exchange came into operation. This had required the construction of the massive tower alongside the Relief Road, which many still consider an eyesore. It is ironic that only twenty or so years later, when electronic telephones and exchange equipment came into use, only a tiny fraction of the space provided by that building would be required.

Of course, the major telephonic change affecting Newbury has been the advent of mobile phone technology. The commercial application of this is owed to a Newbury company. Vodafone was initially an offshoot of Racal, but in 1991 it became an independent company. It expanded rapidly and eventually acquired 50 separate offices before moving into its new headquarters at Shaw in 2002.

Vodafone's early offices were at 20-22, The Broadway, from where the first public mobile phone call in the UK was received – from London – on 1 January 1985. The phone used was a VT1 (shown here). It cost £1,650, gave 30 minutes talk time, and weighed around 5 kg. But for phone users, you could now be In when you were Out!

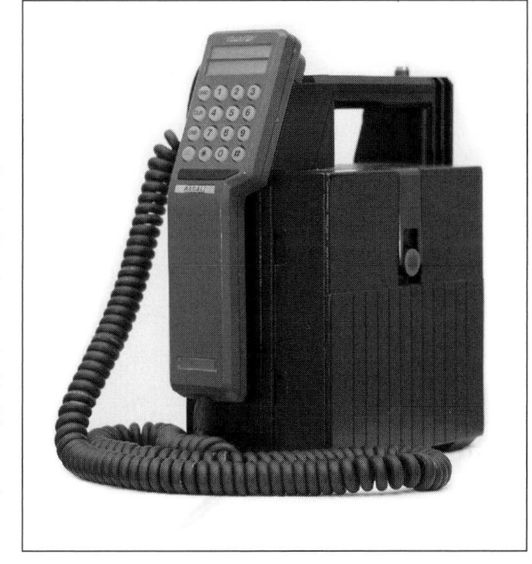

Housing, Shops and Churches

Like all towns, Newbury has experienced great change in the past sixty years. Industrial businesses have moved from the town centre or closed down, making space for shops and offices. In the 1960s houses and cottages in the town centre were demolished as sub-standard, or converted to business use. In contrast, in the past decade or so flats have been created above shops or by the conversion of office buildings to bring life back into the town. Away from the centre, large areas have been developed for housing estates and the sites of larger houses and gardens have been developed with several houses – for example in Andover Road and Speen Lane. Modernisation of public services, such as the sites of the two Newbury Hospitals and Newbury College in Oxford Road, also left plots now developed with housing, as did the site of Turnpike School after its pupils were transferred either to Thatcham or the new Trinity School adjoining Shaw House. A substantial number of flats and houses have also been built at Newbury racecourse.

Large areas proposed for housing are always controversial, but currently an application to build several thousand homes on a greenfield site between Wash Common and the A339 at Sandleford has raised a great deal of opposition. An unusual point in this case is that there is a good claim that the land is a 'Capability' Brown landscape, associated with Elizabeth Montagu of Sandleford Priory.

Shopping has become a major activity. Whilst in the 1960s many shops were still small, specialist, locally-owned businesses, now almost all shops are part of national or international chains. Large new shopping centres have been developed, firstly the Kennet Mall/Shopping Centre in the 1970s and 1980s, then, in the 1990s out-of-town at Pinchington Lane, and most recently, in 2011, Parkway. Large stores have also been developed eastwards along London Road.

The out of town development at Pinchington Lane began with the building of a Hilton hotel and large Tesco supermarket – in January 1991. At the same time Tesco closed their supermarket in Northbrook Street, but opened a smaller shop on the opposite side, where they still are. The Pinchington Lane store was enlarged to become a Tesco Extra. In 1996 many of the town's major car dealers began their move to the Motor Park, adjacent to Tesco and 1997 saw the opening of Newbury Retail Park nearby. Other car dealers remained nearer the town in the Faraday Road/London Road area.

Pedestrianisation of the town's main streets, the Market Place and Parkway have prompted the growth of open air cafes – an extension of indoor areas. There are now many more eating places, offering a variety of menus, compared with twenty years ago – let alone sixty.

Regular attendance at church and chapel has declined and a number have merged and /or been demolished. Contrary to this pattern, the Roman Catholics built a new church at Wash Common – St Francis De Sales.

Newbury from the south, 1960s. Cheap Street can be seen with a mass of buildings where the Kennet Centre is now. The larger roofs belong to Plenty's Eagle Ironworks, where a range of equipment and fittings was produced for agricultural, industrial and domestic uses. Early coastal lifeboats were invented and made here in 1816. Plenty's moved to Hambridge Road in 1965. The prominent building near St Nicolas' church is the Regal cinema, later demolished for the building of the Pearl Assurance building. *(photographer not known)*

Part of Elliotts of Newbury's premises can be seen occupying a large area behind the Methodist Chapel in Northbrook Street and across the area now called Strawberry Hill. Elliotts made good quality furniture and, until the mid-1960s, high performance gliders. They moved from Newbury in 1974 and closed soon afterwards. At their post-war peak (1960s) they had employed over 500 people. *(photographer not known)*

One local entrepreneur who received both praise and criticism for property development through his firm Trencherwood New Homes, was John Norgate. Both Henwick sports fields and Newbury Rugby Club's current site owe their existence to him. The former in return for permission to build at Dunston Park and the latter in exchange for their former ground in Pinchington Lane where part of Newbury Retail Park was built. A developer from further afield is unlikely to have so readily ploughed money into local facilities.

John Norgate, sadly he died at a young age in October 1995. *Photo courtesy Mrs D Norgate*

Flats on the site of Town Mills were built by Trencherwood in 1981. A hotel had originally been proposed for the site, but after it had changed hands several times and lain waste for almost a decade it was bought by Trencherwood and the current flats built. *(publisher)*

Housing

Houses in Jack Street (behind Marks and Spencer) just before they were demolished in 1962. *Chris Hall – West Berkshire Museum 1995.72.36*

Cottages in Brixton Rise, off Cheap Street, demolished around 1960. The same maltings buildings seen in the railway goods yard photograph (see page 31) are beyond the end of the terrace. *Chris Hall – West Berkshire Museum 1995.72.33*

Trafalgar Place, off Bartholomew Street, 1960. Not all cottages demolished in this era were run-down. *Chris Hall – West Berkshire Museum 1995.72.41*

Battledene, off Andover Road. *Courtesy of Dave Stubbs*
The roadway curving down from the house is more-or-less on the line of Glendale Avenue. The Wash Common housing estate was built in the 1970s largely on the land belonging to two or three very large houses, to the west side of Andover Road.

Flats above Parkway shopping centre, with views over Victoria Park, in 2016 *(author)*

Sundial House on the corner of Cheap Street and the Relief Road, built as offices in the 1980s and converted to flats in 2015, as was its companion building Clock House. *(author)*

Shops

Flower House corner, 1969. Rebuilt in the early 1980s. This was at the corner of London Road and The Broadway. *West Berkshire Museum 2004.50.541*

1 to 3 London Road, in 1969. They were small businesses which had probably lost some of their customers due to demolition of nearby cottages. *West Berkshire Museum 2004.50.552*

Halfords, 64/65 Northbrook Street. This wonderful exuberant structure was built for Joseph Hopson in 1877 but demolished by Halfords in 1968 and replaced by the present structure. (now Metro bank) *West Berkshire Museum 2004.50.587*

Invicta Bookshop, Cromwell Place (off Northbrook Street), started by Peter Hall around 1970 and continued by his two sons, Tim (shown here) and Simon. One always wondered how they managed to cram so many second-hand books into two small former cottages. The shop closed about 2010 and is still missed by many. *Jim Irving*

Northbrook Street, 1960s. Burton's tailors were a popular supplier of reasonably priced made-to-measure suits for men at a time when any male office worker and many shop workers were expected to wear a suit. The building is now Halifax Building Society. *David Canning*

Northbrook Street 2016. The left hand section of the Boots building used to be Timothy Whites, chemists, and the right hand section was Boots. After the two companies merged in the 1970s, the shops were rebuilt as the Boots premises open today. *Publisher*

Boots windows in 1960. *David Canning*

Camp Hopson, Park Way entrance 2016. *(author)*

Camp Hopson, furniture department 2016. *(author)*

Camp Hopson's (opposite page) was created from the merger of two local companies in 1921 and was the leading store for many generations of shoppers. Around 2000 the body of the store was completely remodelled, producing a rear facade accessed from Park Way and adjacent to the future Parkway shopping development. A separate furniture department was built in 1998, overlooking the river. The local ownership was lost in 2014 when the company was sold to Morley's Stores Ltd., a larger family-run business. The shop was again re-modelled in 2016.

Bendy's and Heather's stores looking southwards up Bartholomew Street just prior to their demolition, along with The Regal cinema, to allow the building of the Pearl Assurance building. In 2016, planning permission was given for the demolition of the Pearl building and its replacement by flats with shops below. *West Berkshire Museum 2000.20.66*

Shops in Bartholomew Street, opposite Craven Road. They were demolished in the 1960s for the building of Maidenhead House office block. *West Berkshire Museum 1996.125.58*

Cheap Street looking south, in 1967. Whilst St Mary's almshouses (on the right) have since been demolished and Blue Cross has gone, the Empire Cafe continues, see opposite. *(photographer not known)*

The Empire Café and bakery claims to be Newbury's oldest locally-owned business. It has remained in the same family since 1947. *Publisher*

The same premises in the 1930s: there had been a bakery at this building since 1874. The café and bakery flourished during the time the cattle market occupied the site behind it. The large upper room of the café was known as the Farmer's Room and was well used by them. The back doors were always open so they could walk straight in. *(Courtesy of Wendy Berkeley)*

Welcome Café, 49/50, Cheap Street, 1972. This 17th century building is little changed, but the cafe has long gone. *Jack Hole – West Berkshire Museum 2004.50.467*

Daniel's Store, 25/27, Market Place, 1972/3, the shop still had an 'island window', prior to its remodelling. The interiors of the shops were again remodelled in 2016. *Jack Hole – West Berkshire Museum 2004.50.484*

Hickman & Son and Oxfam shop, Market Place (Immediately to the left of Daniel's), 1972/3. Oxfam was one of very few charity shop in Newbury at this date: they were sometimes allowed use of empty shops rent-free. *Jack Hole – West Berkshire Museum 2004.50.482.1*

Laundrette, Queens Road c 1970. At a time when fewer people had their own washing machines – or the space for them – laundrettes were popular, though one had to wait a long time for the washing cycle to be completed. Some shops offered a service whereby an assistant would, for a fee, put in and take out your laundry, others were not staffed, but coin operated. *Jim Irving*

The Kennet Centre

This development by Ravenseft in the early 1970s resulted in the demolition of a large number of Newbury's older buildings and a complete remodelling of the southern part of the town centre. The remaining photographs in this section relate to that development.

The recent construction of Parkway shopping centre also led to the clearance of a very large area including a number of old buildings, but it has had less effect on the street frontage of Northbrook Street than The Kennet Centre had on Bartholomew Street and Cheap Street, as the following photographs show.

Building of The Kennet Centre under way in 1974, as seen across Cheap Street from the Telecom tower. The large office block to the left of the centre of the photo is Maidenhead House, just above it to the left is St Nicolas school in Enborne Road. *Jim Irving*

The Walkway from Bartholomew Street to Cheap Street (the gables of the Post Office can be seen in the background) which existed from the end of the first phase of the Kennet Centre until preparations were being made for the 1984 remodelling and extension of the centre. This first stage also included a children's playground with swings etc. *Jim Irving*

House behind 25, Cheap Street being demolished in December 1970. The house contained the room where, in 1643, Lord Falkland reputedly took Communion on the eve of the First Battle of Newbury. *Brian Coghlan – West Berkshire Museum. 2004.50.092*

Cheap Street about 1968, a year or two before the buildings to the right of the castellated Catherine Wheel were demolished. The properties behind Penn's shoe shop have already gone. The building to become Barclays Bank is under construction to the right; it opened in September 1969. The Post Office yard is in left foreground. *(photographer not known)*

Bartholomew Street, from Market Street, 1970/71. The only building still standing on the east side – and that was soon to go – is number 121. This stood immediately south of the Nias garage and was a Listed Building. It was of 17th or early 18th century date with an 18th century frontage and 18th century wooden panelling in one room. – *West Berkshire Museum 2000.20.135*

Bartholomew Street, east side, and north from the Bricklayers Arms (now The Newbury), about 1970. The shops immediately north of the pub were demolished soon afterwards. – *West Berkshire Museum 2000.20.136*

Bartholomew Street, east side, looking north from Herborough House, occupied by Nias garage, which appears to be empty, about 1970. Herborough House was the home of Walter Money, the founder of modern Newbury historical studies in the late 19th century. – *West Berkshire Museum 2000.20.134*

Open square within the Kennet Centre. *Jim Irving – West Berkshire Museum 2003.46.3*

A glimpse of the murals (opposite page) can be seen behind the shoppers with their Sainsbury's trolleys, about 1985. *Jim Irving*

The same square (oppostie page) roofed over in phase two. The murals painted onto the wall of the extended Sainsbury's store can be seen, about 1985. *Jack Hole – West Berkshire Museum 1999.11.21*

Churches and Chapels

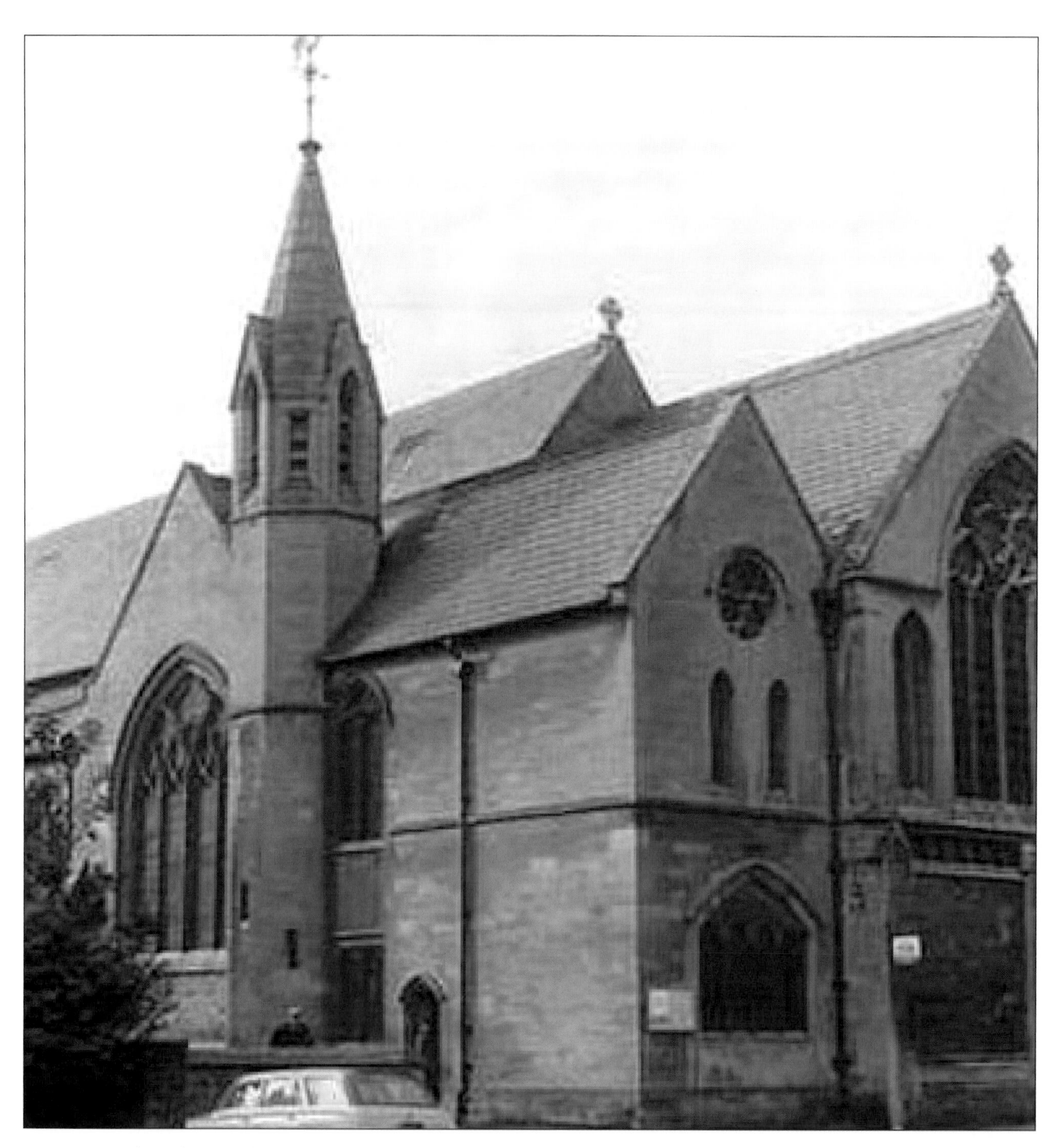

St Mary's Church, London Road c 1970. The church had closed by this time and it was demolished in 1976. A doctor's surgery and flats were built on its site. *(photographer not known)*

Interior of St Mary's shortly before its demolition in 1976. *West Berkshire Museum 2004.50.661*

St Hilda's Mission Church (C of E), 1965. Sited at the corner of Salcombe Road and Fifth Road and demolished in the 1980s. Houses are now on its site. *Jim Irving*

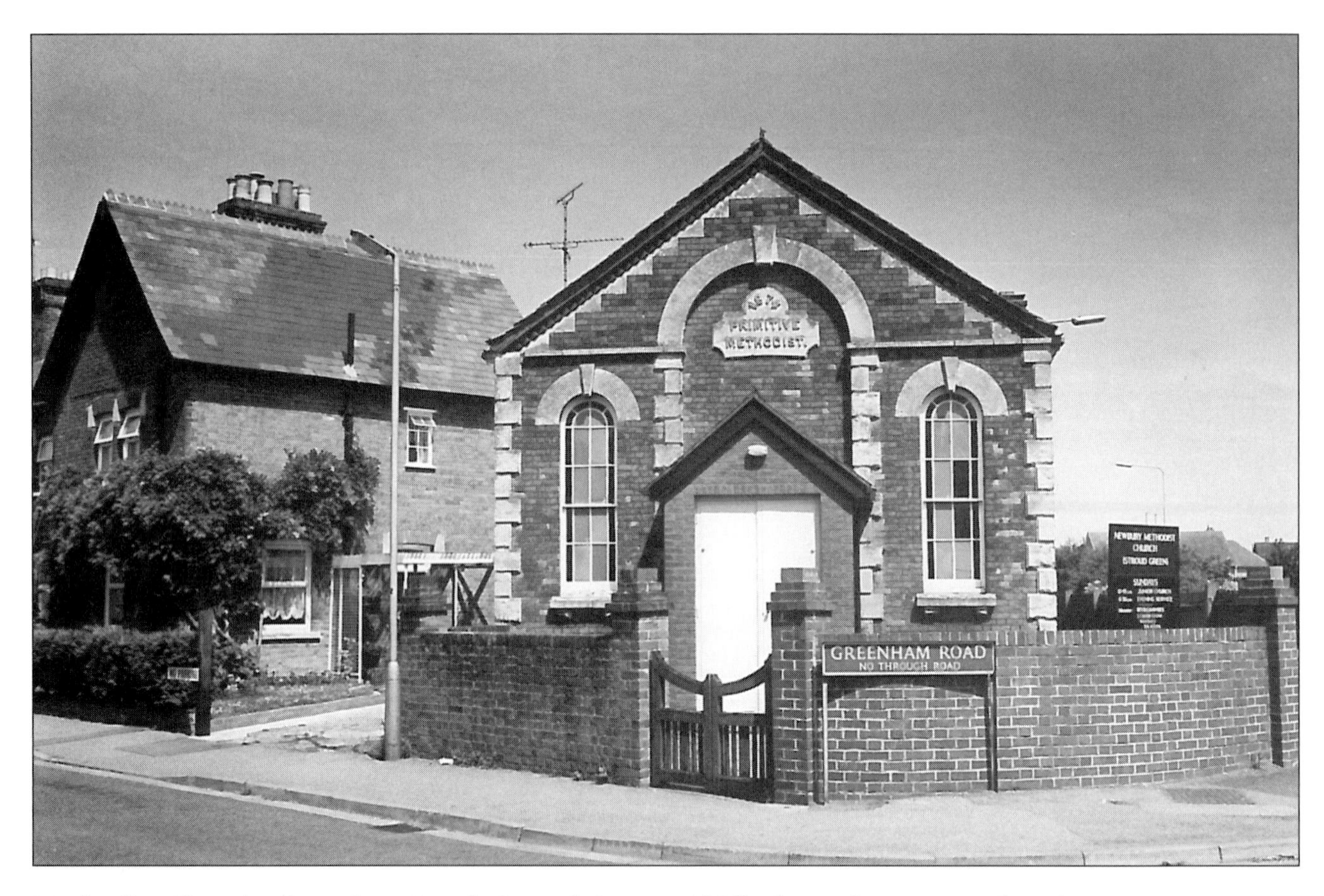

Methodist Church, Greenham Road, Stroud Green, 1986, about the time it closed. *Jim Irving – West Berkshire Museum D3995a*

The same building in 2016; still providing excellent accommodation. *Publisher*

Employment

In the 1960s there were still companies manufacturing products in, or only just outside, the town centre. Plenty's engineering company had been established between Cheap Street and Bartholomew Street since the end of the 18th century and stayed there until 1965, when they moved to new premises in Hambridge Road. They still manufacture equipment, but now trade as part of SPX Flow Technology. Newbury Diesel Company manufactured diesel engines – from small ones for factory or farm to large units for coastal shipping – in King's Road, where Sainsbury's petrol station is now sited. In 1967, when they changed to making ships' remote control gear, they no longer needed heavy engineering facilities and moved to premises in Cyril Vokins Road, off Hambridge Lane in 1981. Eventually, they were sold to Radamec and still operate from the same premises as Radamec Control Systems Ltd. Elliotts of Newbury made high quality furniture in extensive works to the west of the Methodist Church in Northbrook Street. They were the town's largest employer in the 1950s and 60s, but contracted in size and moved from Newbury in 1974. Bayer's former offices are on much of their former site and the Northcroft housing estate is also built on their land. There were, and still are, other engineering companies and manufacturers of equipment in the industrial estates. Other businesses in the town included a milk processing, bottling and distribution depot behind Bartholomew Street, and several maltings.

Newbury Diesel Company's works are at the top of this photograph, most prominent are the workshops of Nias garage. The eastern side of Winchcombe Road can be seen, the rest having been demolished for the Relief Road. All this has now gone and Sainsbury's occupies the site. *Photographer not known*

Sterling Cables premises in King's Road on the former gasworks site. The tall building is basically the gasworks retort tower, extended higher. *Jim Irving*

Sterling Cables manufactured high-quality electrical cables for specialist purposes, such as naval ships, oil rigs, oil refineries and airports. They had premises at Aldermaston as well as in the former gas works buildings in Kings Road. The Newbury base was closed in the 1980s and the Aldermaston factory soon afterwards. The Kings Road site has been used as a small industrial estate, but planning permission has now been granted for demolition of the buildings on the site and erection of housing. A new road will be incorporated to allow traffic to travel from Sainsbury's and Mole Country Stores, beneath the Boundary Road bridge and join Hambridge Road.

Many of these businesses have moved or closed and Newbury's main employment is now IT or office-based. Merchant bankers Kleinwort Benson moved a section of their administration to 'The Lawn', Old Bath Road in 1958, employing about 20 staff. In the 1970s they had built a large angled extension to the property and employed over 300 staff. The office closed in 1991, with most staff being transferred to their London base. In 1981, Bayer plc, the international pharmaceutical and chemical company, moved their UK and Ireland headquarters to newly-built offices on Elliotts site. Sadly, in 2016 they announced that they were to move to the Reading outskirts. By far the largest employer now is Vodafone. The company started in Newbury in 1985 as a subsidiary of Racal, but became independent in 1991 and quickly developed. It built its headquarters on a greenfield site at Shaw and its staff began their transfer to the new building – from over fifty separate offices – in 2002. In 2016 about 5,700 staff are employed at Shaw and two other bases in Newbury.

Snell building in Turnpike Road, formerly the home of Quantel and built in the 1940's to house a Vickers-Armstrong factory manufacturing aircraft sections. *Author*

Other late 20th century industries are electronics, computer programming and data managing; several companies employ highly-skilled scientists and technicians. Perhaps the best-known of these is Quantel, now absorbed into Snell Advanced Media. Quantel (founded in 1973) led the world in the digitisation, manipulation and storage of visual images for television, film and other purposes. From the same premises in Turnpike Road Snell continues to develop equipment for similar purposes and for live transmission of images. Their equipment and software have been used in many major films using CGI effects. Now the largest IT company based in Newbury is Micro Focus International. Although started in London in 1976, it moved its head office to Newbury in 1983. In the early 1990s it moved into the former office of Kleinwort Benson, (between Old Bath Road and the A4) which it remodelled. It produces infrastructure software for a global market. In September 2016 it announced a merger with a section of Hewlett Packard Enterprise, turning it into a multi-billion pound company.

Hambridge Road. The Horizon West estate being built in the 1990s. The Harcross building just beyond the new structures is now Jewsons and the new building to its right is Wickes. It was formerly Stryker and the photo itself has been shot from the site of the current (2016) Stryker building. See next page.
Jim Irving – West Berkshire Museum 1995.65.27

Newbury Business Park is in a large, leafy and somewhat hidden site on the A4 (near B&Q) and by the River Lambourn. Regional offices of well-known companies are there, as well as data management and hi-tech firms (including Vodafone). Employment is also provided by the many technical, service, sales, storage and distribution businesses in the industrial estates of Faraday Road, Bone Lane, Hambridge Road and Hambridge Lane. New Greenham Park will be described in a later section.

Stryker UK, with its headquarters in Hambridge Road, is a section of an international company which markets and distributes a broad range of medical products and equipment for orthopaedics and other medical specialities. Stryker moved to its new headquarters building in 2011. *Author*

Public Services

In the 1960s Newbury was governed by a combination of Newbury Borough Council and Berkshire County Council. In 1974, this changed as part of a national reorganisation of local services. Newbury Borough, Newbury RDC (Rural District Council), Hungerford RDC and Bradfield RDC were abolished and the areas of all four merged, with the addition of part of Wantage RDC, to form Newbury District Council. This new council was responsible for just over half of the geographical area of Berkshire. The former northern part of Berkshire (including Wantage and Abingdon) was transferred to Oxfordshire. A further

Phoenix House, Bartholomew Street, had been the offices of Newbury RDC, but from 1974 it housed the District Council's housing department, until the housing stock was sold to an independent organisation now called Sovereign Housing. *West Berkshire Museum 2003.46.21*

reorganisation in 1998 abolished Berkshire County Council, and the Newbury District area was made a unitary authority, responsible for all council services and renamed West Berkshire District Council.

The former proud Newbury Borough found itself without a role in 1974, it didn't even have a strengthened Parish Council, as had every other civil parish in the District. The District Councillors representing the wards of the former Borough formed a group called Newbury Charter Trustees, whose duties were largely ceremonial, preserving some of the traditions of the Borough. They were allowed to use some of the space in Newbury Town Hall. This changed in 1997 when the District Council authorised the formation of Newbury Town Council and ceded to it some of its responsibilities, including management of Victoria Park, allotments, Newbury Town Hall and the market. In common with other parish councils the Town Council was able to add a precept to the council tax of its residents and its comments on planning applications being considered by the District Council had now to be taken into formal consideration.

In 1974 several departments of the new council were housed in Mill Reef House, Cheap Street, but other buildings were also used including the Town Hall, offices in Wharf Road and Phoenix House, mentioned opposite. *West Berkshire Museum 2003.46.20*

Newbury District Council built offices in Market Street (opened 1982) to bring together their staff distributed around several buildings in the town, principally those mentioned on the previous page. Following the abolition of Berkshire County Council in 1998, the offices were again inadequate and many new buildings were used. New practices, where services are contracted out to other organisations, mean that fewer officers are now needed. *Author*

The enlargement of Thames Valley Police Newbury headquarters in 1974. *Jim Irving*

The police force had been a county responsibility until 1968 when it was merged with others to form Thames Valley Police. The county council had built a new police station in Mill Lane in 1965/7, and in 1974 an additional floor and northern extension were added to make new Divisional headquarters. The courthouse was also built in 1965, adjoining the police station; this was closed in 2016 as part of a government scheme to merge courts. A new Fire and Ambulance Station had been built in Hawthorn Road in the late 1950s.

Computer based book issues, 1994. *Jim Irving – West Berkshire Museum 1995.65.4*

Newbury Library in Cheap Street was extended by the Borough in 1968, but by the time computer issuing of books had been introduced it was a Berkshire County service. The County drew up plans for a new library on Greenham Wharf, but by the time it was completed on 31st July 2000 it was run by West Berkshire Council. The Cheap Street site is now Prezzo restaurant.

Park House School, Wash Common, 1980. *(courtesy Jim Irving)*

Park House School began as a boys secondary modern in 1947 after the county bought the house which gave it its name, just seen at the left of the photo. It became a mixed comprehensive school in 1975 and its facilities gradually expanded . A large sports hall was built in the 1980's with a substantial contribution to its costs by Newbury District Council in return for its facilities being made available for public use out of school hours. The school became a specialist sports college in 1998 and achieved academy status in 2011.

The fine Elizabethan mansion of Shaw House had been used as a school since its emergency use following the bombing of the Newbury Council School in 1943. After the war the building was purchased from its private owners by the County Council and from 1947 became a girls' secondary modern school, and then a mixed comprehensive school in 1975. Additional buildings had been added, but in 1982 the mansion was vacated after fairly serious structural faults were discovered and the pupils moved into temporary

The main entrance front of Shaw House, shrouded in scaffolding during its major restoration. The whole house was surrounded with scaffold, including a 'roof' to keep the building watertight while the tiles were removed. *West Berkshire Council*

buildings. In 1999 the school was merged with Turnpike School (which was demolished), and the new combined school became Trinity School. Further permanent buildings have been added, particularly to enable it to carry out its function as a specialist music and performing arts academy.

The important historic building remained unused for many years until a National Lottery award and other funding was found to carry out the major restoration needed. Shaw House was opened to the public in 2008. One wing is used to explain the building's history, Newbury Registry Office is based there and the house is an attractive place for weddings. Other rooms are available for public hire or used for other council purposes. An annual programme of events is also arranged.

There have been other changes to education provision. At the end of 1989, Victoria Park Nursery School moved from wartime buildings in the centre of the park to a purpose-built facility at its northern edge. Several primary schools have also been built or rebuilt. St Bartholomew's Grammar School for Boys and the County Girls' Grammar School first merged to become a comprehensive school in 1975 and, in 2010 moved into brand

Shaw House from the east, 2016. *Publisher*

new buildings, sited between the former schools. The following year they were granted academy status. The old buildings have been converted into flats. What was The South Berks. College of Further Education became Newbury College in 1975, and in 2002 moved to new buildings in Monk's Lane. Its former site in Oxford Road has been redeveloped with flats and houses.

Newbury District Hospital stood in Andover Road from its opening in 1885. It was extended on various occasions until its closure and demolition in 2004, when it was replaced by the new West Berkshire Community Hospital in Turnpike Road. Sandleford Hospital, which provided geriatric and maternity services was closed at the same time and its services, too, transferred to the new hospital. *West Berkshire Museum. 1998.13.13*

Arts, Entertainments and Sport

The Corn Exchange had provided a space for town events from its opening in 1862. A remodelling of the interior had taken place in the 1950s, but in 1988 these additions were considered a fire risk. Structural problems were also found and the building was closed. In 1991 Newbury District Council decided it should be restored and improved and in September 1993 it reopened as an arts venue. It now presents a regular programme of widely varied events – popular music, classical music, dramatic performances, comedy, film and much more. In 2000, the Council delegated its management to an independent trust; a procedure adopted for a number of its services. Whilst it has continued with its programme of events, the Corn Exchange has in addition promoted regular, free, 'street theatre' events each summer, which have drawn audiences of thousands. It has also taken on the management of New Greenham Arts and acted as a ticket agency for other local organisations.

It is difficult to illustrate the Plaza as it has no street frontage, access was via a passageway from the Market Place. The theatre had been started as a private venture by Jimmy Tufnail in 1925, but acquired by the Borough Council in 1933. It had a stage topped by a fly tower to allow the scenery to be lifted above the stage and had a sprung dance floor, a superior feature.

Whilst a little outside the town, Arlington Arts at Snelsmore, also provides a range of high-quality performances, but with a different emphasis to the Corn Exchange. The Watermill Theatre at Bagnor has a regional and national reputation for its year-round programme of professionally acted new and classic plays, plus musicals and youth theatre productions.

Wrestling was a popular entertainment in the 1960s and 70s and had a regular spot on television. Programmes of wrestling bouts were staged at both the Plaza and Corn Exchange. Both venues housed a variety of events, including banquets and dancing as well as theatre and pop concerts. During the 1960's groups such as The Who, Jimmy Hendrix, Cream and The Pretty Things played in those places.

In the late seventies the Plaza was leased to a company who planned to convert it into a night club. Before this was carried out there was a very cold winter but the central heating system had not been drained and the pipes burst. The subsequent thaw saw the

Corn Exchange, 1972/3. The ball finials to the pediment were removed as unsafe around 1980. *Jack Hole – West Berkshire Museum 2004.50.475*

building flooded and the dance floor distorted and ruined. A few years later the Plaza and the building fronting the Market Place were sold and demolished for the building of new offices for Dreweatt, Watson and Barton, which opened around 1985.

In the 1940s Newbury still had three cinemas, but the Carlton ('Flea Pit'), Cheap Street, burnt down in 1950 and the Regal, Bartholomew Street, closed in 1962, leaving only the Forum in Park Way. This then operated under different names until it closed in November 1998, and is now BST Fitness. For 11 years townspeople either travelled to places such as Basingstoke or relied on films staged at the Corn Exchange until, in 2009, the Vue cinema was built on the former surface car park of the Kennet Centre.

The Arts Workshop in Northcroft Lane provided a range of courses, exhibitions, dramatic performances, poetry and music recitals from 1978 until 1998 when it closed. A similar venture then opened, New Greenham Arts, as part of the redevelopment of the former military base. This venue also provides several workshops for hire by artists. The museum regularly showed art exhibitions as part of its exhibition programme until the end of the 20th century. The Corn Exchange used its entrance way for art exhibitions for several years after its reopening in 1993. For varying periods there have been craft shops in the

Plaza Theatre, entrance from Market Place, 1970s. *Jim Irving*

town which have staged exhibitions, and in 2014 City Arts opened in Hampton Road. This is a privately owned community arts hub and stages innovative arts events, art and craft instruction and exhibitions.

Open Studios is an annual event, begun in 1988 by the late Pat Eastop MBE, when artists and craftspeople stage displays of their work, often in their workshops, but also in joint displays. Most of the work is for sale and the scheme gives an opportunity to buyers and

Plaza Theatre, wrestling, 1970s. *Jim Irving*

visitors to discuss with artists the inspiration for their work. The success of the scheme has led to its coverage extending for almost 20 miles around Newbury.

However, the major provider of top quality musical performances since it inception in 1978, has been Newbury Spring Festival. Each May, national and international performers provide two weeks of concerts, recitals and spoken events at venues in Newbury and the surrounding area.

In 1937, a lido was developed from a less formal swimming area formed from a branch

Northcroft Recreation Centre, children's pool with the adult pool beyond soon after its opening. *West Berkshire Museum 2003.46.16*

of the River Kennet, which then flowed across Northcroft and Goldwell Park. Further improvements were made in 1963, including adding a paddling pool. In 2016 there was a renewed national interest in lidos, perhaps in view of the hot summer enjoyed that year. Newbury's lido has always been a local attraction in good weather, but if fine summers continue it may attract a wider clientele.

There had been public support in the 1970s for an indoor pool to be created and a local lottery was set up to try and raise the cost. However, Newbury District Council decided to finance the building of indoor pools and squash courts, which opened in 1980. A few years later, a large sports hall and other facilities were added. Soon afterwards, management of the centre was let to a commercial company following government pressure for local authorities to delegate management of their facilities.

Northcroft Park provides space for informal recreation as well as football pitches and the home of Newbury Cricket and Hockey Clubs. The annual Michaelmas funfair is held here, its name a last link with one of the ancient fairs which once aided the medieval town's prosperity.

During the 1980s the District Council planned to improve recreational facilities across west Berkshire in addition to the Northcroft Recreation Centre. In Newbury, this included a large contribution to the building of a new sports hall at Park House School (then a Berkshire education committee school) in return for public access during out of school hours. Similarly, a major grant was made to West Berkshire Indoor Bowls Club to enable them to build new premises at Greenham, again in return for public access.

Newbury Rugby Club benefited from the development value of their ground in Pinchington Lane. Trencherwood provided them with a new clubhouse and pitches in Monk's Lane in 1996, and were then able to develop the previous grounds with Newbury Retail Park. Newbury Football Club's pitch was moved to its present site due to the building of the Relief Road and development of the London Road Industrial Estate. In 2016, the club signed a two year lease, but will then have to leave the ground as its site is needed for the redevelopment of the industrial estate. The District Council provides many recreational pitches in and around Newbury for non-professional clubs. The largest facility is at Henwick Worthy Field, opened in 1996, which was originally provided by Trencherwood in return for planning permission to build houses at Dunston Park, Thatcham.

Golf is a sport which has grown in popularity during the past 35 years. Newbury & Crookham Golf Club is long-established, and there are now three others in the immediate area of the town. Newbury Racecourse Golf Club closed in May 2016, after more than 20 years, as the land it occupied was required for the Racecourse redevelopment.

Newbury Racecourse is a major national venue for the sport and also helps identify the town to outsiders. Whilst it holds both Flat and National Hunt races on 30 days throughout the year, the highlight of the Jump programme is focussed on The Hennessy Gold Cup, held each November. The main Flat meeting is the Al Shaqab Lockinge Stakes – worth £350,000 – held in May.

In the final decade of the 20th century, substantial improvements to the racecourse

West Berkshire Indoor Bowls Club, 1980s. *Jim Irving*

were made by replacing the old stands with large modern buildings incorporating conference and exhibition spaces and restaurants. In August 2016, a £20m phase of redevelopment of the course's facilities began. This brings new facilities for owners and trainers, a hostel for Jockeys and space for saddling and parading the horses. The new bridge from Hambridge Road has already been mentioned (see page 24). The bridge gives direct access to a large coach park and internal roads lead to the fitness centre, the flats and a new eastern entrance to the racecourse.

The racecourse owns a very large acreage and parts of it are, not without controversy, being developed with 1500 flats and houses. There is also the large health and fitness centre, complete with swimming pool. This non-racing activity is justified by the need to raise income to offset the costs of racing and keep facilities up-to-date.

The Berkshire Stand and Grandstand at Newbury Racecourse, September 2016. *Author*

Flats being built at Newbury Racecourse, September 2016. *Publisher*

Greenham Common

The Common was purchased by the Borough of Newbury when it was put up for sale in 1938, even though it was in an adjacent parish, as it recognised the enjoyment and exercise Newbury people had enjoyed there for many years. Early in the 1939-45 war the Common was commandeered for use as an RAF airfield. After the war it was anticipated that it would be released back to community use, but in 1951 a scheme was announced for the Air Ministry to acquire most of Greenham and Crookham commons for the creation of a heavy bomber base for the US Air Force. The runway was one of the longest in Europe. It was used as a bomber base until 1964 when it became a standby base.

USAF B47 Stratojet of the type based at Greenham Common until 1964. The planes were so heavy that, when bombed up, they needed boosters known as JATO bottles (seen here) to shorten the runway take-off distance. *Wikepedia*

Silos for the nuclear Cruise missiles at Greenham Common. *Photographer not known*

Cruise missile being fired from mobile rocket launcher. *Photographer not known*

Sitting around a fire alongside an entrance to Greenham airbase. *West Berkshire Museum 1988.3.3*

Then in 1981 it was chosen as a base for USAF Cruise Missiles which were to be armed with nuclear warheads. This brought opposition and the Greenham Common Women's Peace Camps around the base developed from a peace march 'Women for Life on Earth' from Cardiff to Greenham, which arrived early in September 1981 and then stayed. The women constantly tried to disrupt the work to strengthen the fences around the base and build the silos to house the missile convoys. In turn, the women would be evicted, their camps destroyed and possessions removed. Many women were arrested and imprisoned.

Possessions prepared for moving to prevent the bailiffs taking them. *West Berkshire Museum 1988.3.17*

The first of an eventual 106 missiles arrived in November 1983. Eventually, following the Intermediate-range Nuclear Weapons Treaty between USA and USSR, the cruise missiles were returned to the USA to be destroyed, the final ones leaving Greenham in March 1991. The last of the US forces left the base in September 1992.

The Ministry of Defence announced the sale of the airfield in 1993 – apart from the silo area which was subject to Russian inspection to confirm it was unused. In March 1997,

Breaking up the runway. *Peter Bloodworth, West Berkshire Museum 1995.63*

David Rendel MP holding the pair of wire-cutters he had used to symbolically cut down the final stretch of perimeter fencing on 8th April 2000. *Peter Bloodworth, West Berkshire Museum 2001.10.1*

the whole common was sold to Greenham Common Trust for seven million pounds. The same day the Trust sold the whole area, apart from the built up part south of the runway, to Newbury District Council for £1. The built up area was renamed New Greenham Park and converted to commercial use, the profits from this to go to local causes. Initially much of the income was spent on restoring the common. This included removing massive underground fuel tanks and the runway. Thousands of tons of crushed material from the base were used in embankments for the Newbury by-pass. As the common became safer, the security fence was removed, the last section symbolically by the late David Rendel MP on 8th April 2000. At last the public again had access, as did those with Commoners Rights who wished to graze their cattle there. It was perhaps surprising how quickly nature restored the common.

Greenham Common Trust has renamed the 150 acre commercial area Greenham Business Park, many of the original military buildings have been demolished and replaced and it now has the appearance of a modern business. Since 1997 the Trust has given £32.5 million generated by the rents of property to a great variety of projects in West Berkshire and part of north Hampshire.

Endpiece

Britain in the 1960s and early 70s was keen to leave the past behind and actively embrace a modern, optimistic future. Today, looking back at these photographs, it seems a terrible waste to have lost some of our historic buildings. A 17th century listed house with links to the First Battle of Newbury could never be demolished now. The distinctive row of dwellings on Jack Street, the gothic splendour of the former Halfords in Northbrook Street, and the row of charming cottages in Trafalgar Place; all have disappeared. However, Newbury is a thriving market town that needs to house its growing population and compete with the surrounding region to attract shoppers and visitors. The development at Parkway, smartly fitted into the area between Northbrook Street and Victoria Park, when compared to the destruction beside the market place for the Kennet Centre, was much more sensitively carried out and is proving a welcome addition to the town.

You can sit outside a café in the Market Square, so long as the weather is on your side, and appreciate the majority of the buildings that are shown in this book. While the trees, benches and paving, as well as the lack of cars, have actively improved the area.

There is also another pastime. As you walk down Northbrook Street and Bartholomew Street, why not look up and above the chain store windows? You will see that much of old Newbury is still there to be admired.

Acknowledgements

I would like to thank everyone who has assisted in the preparation of this book, not least the photographers who took the original photographs and thus provided us with a record of the town. In these days of the internet it is sometimes difficult to identify who the photographer was or who owns the copyright. I therefore apologise to those whose work we haven't been able to acknowledge and ask for their understanding. Anonymous photographs have only been selected when they showed a view that I could not find elsewhere. I would be grateful if copyright owners of any work selected, but not acknowledged, would contact the publisher so that the situation can be corrected in any future edition.

The publishers, Nicholas and Suzanne Battle, have been most supportive during the preparation of the book and been encouraging at every stage, I thank them. Nicholas also took some of the images of Newbury today. The production manager, Martin Marwood, has also been helpful, especially his patience whilst I tied up a number of loose ends. Ruth Paley deserves praise for her copy editing. The majority of the photographs have come from three main sources: the museum, Jim Irving and David Canning.

Jim Irving FRPS has been making a photographic record of Newbury since he came to teach in the town in the early 1950s. He has been a member of Newbury Camera Club since that era and has held all major offices in the Club. He played a major part in providing images for my earlier book, *Newbury in the 1950s*, and was equally helpful when I approached him in connection with this one. Ruth Howard, collections manager for West Berkshire Museum could not have been more helpful and patient. During my many visits, Ruth made space for me to go through the museum catalogue of over 6000 photographs to make an initial list of images, and then helped me to extract the actual prints from storage and scan them for reproduction. David Canning is well-known for his wide knowledge of railways and his images of trains, but for many years he has been taking fine photographs of many aspects of the Newbury area. His work often appears in the *Newbury Weekly News* and as background to weather forecasts on television. He was approached by the publisher and immediately agreed to help. He sent electronic copies of a large selection of images from which I made a selection. My very grateful thanks to all three.

Other people have generously allowed photographs in their possession to be reproduced, these are Mrs Wendy Berkeley, Brian Burgess, Christopher and Hugh Marriage, Mrs Delia Norgate, David Stubbs and Alan Vince. Peter Bloodworth and the Newbury Weekly News freely allowed their copyright images in the museum collections to be used and Geraldine Gardner and Jackie Markham helped provide an image of the newspaper's premises. Jane Frapwell and Danielle Hudspith of Vodafone promptly helped with details of the company's current employment numbers and located a suitable image to represent the first UK mobile telephone call. Again I am very grateful to all of these people. Mrs Sue Hopson has kindly agreed to write an introduction to this book. I thank her and also for her appreciation of ensuring a photographic record of the town is kept for future generations. Around 30 years ago she made generous contributions from the receipts from the sale of her own books to ensure the museum photographs were properly stored.

Finally, I cannot forget Kath, my wife, who has been understanding of the amount of time I have spent preparing this book, especially as it grew from the initial proposal to which she had concurred with my acceptance. She has put up with my neglect of gardening and domestic tasks and the delaying of our annual holiday. It is fair to say that without her support I could not have written this book.

Tony Higgott
October 2016

INDEX

2016. Market Square on market day. Taken from The Hatchet Inn. *Publisher*